CASE CLOSED: THE COBAIN MURDER

The Killing and Cover Up of Kurt Cobain

Ian Halperin

SOHO Media Publishing

To: Kurt Donald Cobain (1967-1994)

Birds scream at the top of their lungs in horrified hellish rage every morning at daybreak to warn us all of the truth, but sadly we don't speak bird.

KURT COBAIN

PREFACE

Through Kurt I saw the beauty of minimalism and the importance of music that's stripped down - Dave Grohl

Less is more! After having written two books on this subject, this volume's intent is being focused, accurate, and mindful of the new evidence. Instead of being long-winded and risk getting ignored, this volume cuts to the chase. It's about brevity and being brave enough to tell the truth - with the goal of finally getting Kurt Cobain's case reopened and trying to overturn the verdict in his tragic death from suicide to murder.

I focus mostly on new evidence, while regurgitating and scratching on the bare surface some of the old evidence drawn out in my previous works. I've realized the consequences of not being brief can be severe - people tend to draw out of proportion and context quickly. Long-windedness can be perceived as indecisiveness and quickly cost you people's attention, respect and clarity. That's why this work is concise, to the point, without sparing any of the new, uncovered hard evidence. Still, its eye-catching but without the temptations of all the unnecessary phrases and redundancies that have been so well documented in the previous two volumes.

To all the believers - thanks for your unwavering support and trust. Keep going until justice is served. Never back down. To the non believers - your scepticism and mistrust is deeply acknowledged. I kindly urge you, however, not to judge this case on emotion, hearsay or the ubiquitous circulation of falsities and misleading truths. I urge you to keep an open mind and examine the hardcore evidence in this case, not the misadventures of truth that have had a very long history, as they date back to in this case long before the very day Kurt's body was found by an electrician above the garage in the greenhouse of his Lake Washington home in Seattle's Leschi neighborhood.

GRUNGE

The word grunge means grime or dirt. The grunge sound emanated from the nihilism of punk and the head banging ritual of heavy metal. Grunge became synonymous with the alternative bands in the early nineties. With Mudhoney, Nirvana, and Soundgarden leading the way, Grunge eliminated the tawdry keyboard synth laden music of the eighties and put the edge back into the genre of rock'n' roll.

This book alchemizes the spirit of grunge by keeping it real, unplugged, laying everything out without the gloss and glamor major publishers insist on. Imperfect - but truthful and powerful.

PROLOGUE

It's been almost thirty years since the voice of a generation, Kurt Donald Cobain, was found dead in the greenhouse above the garage in his Lake Washington, Seattle home. This book concludes unwaveringly that Kurt did not commit suicide. He was murdered. It's finally time to get to the bottom of what really happened and to hold those accountable who were involved in Kurt's death. There is no statute of limitations on murder or seeking justice. But with all the new evidence that has come forward, the time is now.

Note - Again, this book I decided to keep raw, unbridled and pure. Nothing fancy - just the evidence. Let the facts roll, in hope the evolution process of this long journey will lead to justice for Kurt.

MURDER

By the time Kurt Cobain was found dead of a shotgun wound in 1994, he had been widely declared the voice of his generation. When that voice was silenced, the shockwaves reverberated with millions of devastated teens throughout the world for whom Cobain was an iconic figure whose music helped them get through their own angst. When it appeared he had killed himself, many felt stunned and betrayed as if their hero had told them not to bother. At least 68 teenagers committed copycat suicides, while tens of thousands of other expressed suicidal feelings to youth hotlines around the world.

When I published my first book with my longtime writing partner Max Wallace, *Who Killed Kurt Cobain*, in 1998, it enabled countless young people make sense of the tragedy and provided a beacon of hope by focusing on the theory — first posited by

Courtney Love's private investigator Tom Grant — that Cobain may not have killed himself after all.

In contrast to the conspiracy theories that often surface after the death of a celebrity, the book provided an objective account of the facts on both sides while taking no stand. The *New Yorker* called the book a "judicious presentation of explosive material."

Six years later, on the tenth anniversary of Cobain's death, we published another book, *Love and Death,* with new evidence suggesting that Cobain may very well have been murdered. By this time, the angst-ridden generation that had mourned Cobain's death had grown up and become part of the book-buying public as evidenced by the book's success around the world where it became an international bestseller in the UK, Japan, Germany, Poland and the Netherlands. The book was launched with an exclusive interview and report on both *Dateline NBC* and the *Today Show* which helped vault it onto the *New York Times* Bestseller list.

In the 20 years since, an entire new generation appears to have discovered Cobain and his music. In the past few years alone, a major feature documentary, *Montage of Heck*, took Sundance by storm and broke box office records for a documentary when it grossed more than $100,000 in a limited two-day theatrical release before it was pulled for release on HBO. In the UK and other countries, the film topped video sales charts and demonstrated Cobain's enormous continuing international appeal. Also in 2015, a Hollywood biopic about Cobain was given the green light with Jared Leto reportedly on board to play Cobain. In the spring of 2016, Lincoln Square Productions — the production house for ABC/Disney — approached me to commission a six-part limited series based on our book, *Love and Death*, which would have undoubtedly provided our investigation with significant credibility and exposure.

Then came Soaked in Bleach, a 2015 docudrama directed by Benjamin Statler. The compelling film was seen through the eyes of Tom Grant, the P.I. who was hired by Courtney Love to find Kurt, shortly before he was found dead in the greenhouse above his garage. The film poked many inconsistencies in the investigation into Kurt's death, raising the question of how he really died and pointed a strong finger toward Kurt's widow Courtney Love. The film combined documentary footage, reenactment of key scenes with actors, and strong interviews with people associated with the case including Seattle Police chief Norm Stamper and world-renowned forensic pathologist Cyril Wecht.

To coincide with the surge of new interest and key new information I obtained , I finally decided I was ready to release a new book, *Case Closed*, which will provide the definitive verdict on what really happened in April 1994 when the voice of a generation was snuffed out.

In the two decades since my first book, I never stopped investigating the case. Although I was an obscure young journalist in 1998, the years since have gained me an international reputation as one of the world's leading chroniclers of celebrity culture. When my book *Unmasked* spent two weeks as a number one *New York Times* bestseller in 2009, it opened significant new doors. Then came my explosive, bestselling book series Controversy: Sex, Lies And Dirty Money By The World's Powerful Elite. The first volume exposed sociopath Jeffrey Epstein's true role procuring young girls for some of the world's most famous names, including Prince Andrew, Bill Clinton and the late Libyan dictator, Muammar Gaddafi. The rest of this series so far includes books about who really broke up The Beatles, how Michael Jackson was a victim of extortion by many who accused him of molesting children and a tell-all about the inner secrets of Hollywood's notorious gay closet. This book is a special edition in the series, becoming Volume 5.

Now, I have uncovered explosive new evidence suggesting that Cobain was not only the victim of foul play but that the Seattle Police Department deliberately covered up evidence proving that they had botched the investigation by declaring Cobain's death an "open and shut case of suicide" less than an hour after his body was found. Giving substantial added weight to my findings is a startling admission by Norm Stamper — Chief of the Seattle Police at the time of Cobain's death. Stamper now admits that his own police force failed to properly investigate the death and is considering to publicly call for a new

4

investigation.

This is only the culmination of a staggering dossier of new evidence that I draw on to definitively prove that Kurt Cobain was murdered in April 1994. For the first time, I have pieced together the crucial details of Cobain's murky final days and hours — during which he went missing after escaping from a Los Angeles drug rehab facility — to make an incontrovertible case. And I found a new key witness who has never become forward. I interviewed him twice in the past few years, once in 2017 and again in 2022. The new evidence he presented to me was mind blowing.

Among the significant new highlights of my investigation:

I tracked down the long elusive heroin addicted nanny, Cali — Michael Dewitt — who Tom Grant had linked to Cobain's death but who had gone underground for years. I located DeWitt living in the Los Angeles neighborhood of Echo Park. Posing as a dog-walker, I hired a friend to befriend DeWitt and discovered some crucial new details about Cobain's last days. He discovered that Courtney Love is still providing DeWitt with financial support. Her investigator Tom Grant goes on the record to declare that this has always been merely a payoff for DeWitt's continued silence. My friend, however, refused to convict DeWitt. He claims after much investigation he concludes DeWitt got caught up - unwillingly - in a situation beyond his control.

"Courtney had power over him and dragged him into this to try to cover her tracks," "Brian" said. "Cali seems harmless. I don't think he's capable of hurting a fly let alone be involved in a coverup murder. It's just not in his DNA. He does whatever Courtney says, that's very clear. But there's a fine line he won't cross. I really don't believe there's evidence to make him complicit in this. It sounds good in theory but the hard evidence is just not there."

Another person I tracked down connected to Cali, an artist who has known Cali for years, disagreed. "He's a sleazebucket," the artist said. "He'd do anything for an extra buck. He'd probably kill his own mother if it meant him leading a better life." I will get to more about Cali a bit later.

More compelling was the findings of America's most prominent forensic pathologist Cyril Wecht who declares that the evidence proves Cobain could not have killed himself. Wecht— former President of the American Academy of Forensic Sciences best known for his work on Robert Kennedy's autopsy and the Manson family murders — concludes that the death was almost certainly a "homicide." Wecht's conclusion normally would be more than enough to finally get the case reopened. But Seattle Police, after all these painstaking years, still turn a blind eye.

"Normally, when you have someone as credible as Wecht to on record and contravene the original verdict, it would be more than enough to at least reopen the case and do a proper investigation," a longtime Seattle Police source told me. "It's clear they won't reopen the case because someone powerful in Seattle is still intent on covering the whole Cobain case up. It's extremely disturbing that after all these years a proper investigation is still being denied. Kurt Cobain's death was never investigated properly. It's long overdue that someone steps up in the Seattle Police Department and takes this more seriously. Otherwise, justice will never be served to Kurt."

"This was more likely a homicide than a suicide," Wecht said in the powerful expose film "Soaked In Bleach". "It just doesn't fit."

Wecht said the grunge star had enough heroin in his system to kill at least five people. "All of the drug paraphernalia was put in a cigar box. Everything was placed back in the cigar box. Cobain then proceeds to take a shotgun and kill himself? It's highly unlikely."

One of my longtime sources in the Seattle Police Department, who retired back in 2013, concurred with Wecht. "It amazes me how clear the evidence is in this particular case," he said. "If one properly examines every piece closely, a grade school kid would be able to determine that this case for some reason was not investigated properly. The Seattle PD for some reason was eager to rush to judgment. The bigger question is why? And who pressured the police to close this case so quickly? It's obvious someone from outside exerted pressure to have this case closed quickly. After reexamining this file, I conclude there's at least nine people who had motivation to get this case closed without a proper investigation. These people ranged from the Seattle County Medical Examiner Nikolas Hartshorne, to people connected to Kurt in the music industry, to drug dealers in Seattle, and most of all to Kurt's wife Courtney Love whom he wanted to divorce. In any murder police and investigators first look at the motive. In this particular case there was a ton of motive to have Kurt killed. Kurt was worth much more dead than alive to many people connected to him. He wanted a divorce, and he wanted to quit the music business. You don't have to be Einstein to figure out what happened here. Incredibly Kurt died just a couple months before OJ Simpson was charged for first-degree murder. He got away with it, even though everyone knew he was guilty. Lots of people got away with murder back then. If Kurt died in the same way today the case would been labeled a murder, not suicide. The evidence is too overwhelming. Incredibly, OJ and Courtney Love share the same July 9th birthday. I don't think it's some strange coincidence. I think it's a reflection of who they really are and what's in their true DNA."

Back in 2005, when I produced a documentary The Cobain Case, Tom Grant gave me access to almost all his tape recordings of secretly recorded conversations between Grant and Courtney's lawyer Rosemary Carroll proving that Cobain was planning to divorce Courtney at the time of his death and that he had prepared a new will cutting Courtney out which had not yet been signed. These recordings were powerful. I included them in the extra footage on the DVD which was distributed by Paramount. One of the execs at Paramount who listened to all the recordings told me back then that just based on those recordings alone, excluding all other evidence, the case should have been reopened.

"The tapes are powerful," he said. "It's beyond anyone's comprehension why the cops would discard such clear, powerful and incriminating evidence. I've produced many true crime films and documentaries over the years. Never have I ever seen such clear cut evidence. The Seattle Police were either paid off or are complete, utter idiots. There's no other explanation to this."

Recently, I found new credit card evidence proving that Kurt had booked two plane tickets for himself and his new girlfriend and that he was planning to leave Seattle and Nirvana the week of his death to start a new life and career away from Courtney and his former band. This has never before been properly confirmed. It goes along with the theory in an exclusive interview I had with the closest person in Kurt's life at the time, his grandfather Leland Cobain. I interviewed Leland twice, once for the second book Love And Death and then again on camera for the documentary The Cobain Case. Both times he spouted the same theory.

"Kurt told me he wanted to start a new life away from Seattle, away from Courtney because he had finally found true, unconditional love with a new girlfriend," Leland said. "He told me multiple times he wanted to divorce Courtney. He was afraid of her. He thought she was out of her mind, had violent tendencies and used his fame to further her own. He thought she was a psychopath. I never heard him talk so bad about anyone. But when it came to Courtney he wasn't at a loss for words.

"He also wanted to quit Nirvana. He didn't like the direction the band was heading. He thought they became somewhat of a sellout. It turned him off. He wanted to keep true to his roots. He thought the band had become too manufactured, losing the angst ridden sonic sound that captured the hearts of an entire generation."

Incredibly, I uncovered evidence that more

than 27 million dollars from Cobain's estate unexplainably went missing at the time when Courtney Love was the guardian of her daughter's share of the estate. Love has publicly claimed that she was the victim of "looters" and that she did "not realize the money was missing until it was too late." For the first time, I got exclusive inside info and went behind the scenes to expose a battle between Kurt's daughter Frances Bean Cobain and her mother in which she filed a successful restraining order in Los Angeles Superior Court against Love and made a number of startling claims, including accusing her mother of causing the death of the family's pets because of her "constant drug use and hoarding." I obtained the explosive court testimony which sheds new light on long-standing rumors surrounding what Frances Bean described as Love's "unstable and chaotic behavior," revealing that the two had gotten into a "physical fight." According to Frances Bean's testimony, her mother "has taken drugs for as long as I can remember. She basically exists now on Xanax, Adderall, Sonata and Abilify, sugar and cigarettes."

This was all corroborated by a former bodyguard of Courtney who became a close friend of mine the past few years. He said Courtney's medicine cabinet in her L.A. home looked like "a pharmaceutical den" that had everything "one shouldn't take". Sadly, he also said that Frances had access to the medicine cabinet and started experimenting with Courtney's drugs. "Courtney essentially enabled her own daughter," he said. "And I think it was deliberate. She wanted to calm France down and get her addicted so Frances would back off of the money trail. If Frances kept pursuing the money trail I truly believe Courtney could have gone to jail. The whole thing was messy. Nobody wanted any part of it. Two bodyguards before me quit. Nobody could handle Courtney. I thought of quitting many times. Courtney was just impossible to be around. She was a walking train wreck."

In March 2016, the Seattle Police Department released new photos of Cobain's shotgun a year after they released never before seen photos of the crime scene. The photos were innocuous. I located a Seattle police detective who confided that the department decided to release the photos in an effort to prove they had nothing to hide. "What is more important," the detective told me, "is the evidence that they deliberately failed to release. They are still sitting on the forensics and the pathology report that go a long way to demonstrating that he didn't take his own life. You have to ask yourself why they released the photos and not those reports. It's because it will make them look extremely bad. They know they screwed up, but they'll never admit it."

One thing I set out to get and finally obtained was damaging new evidence and tape recordings demonstrating that Courtney herself used her influence and connections to suppress police evidence from being made public as part of a two-decade long cover up. I linked this evidence to my own previously disclosed trail linking Courtney to the coroner — Nikolas Hartshorne — who originally declared the death a suicide and who I discovered was Courtney's former boyfriend.

The only way to definitively make this evidence public and to prove once and for all that Cobain was murdered is to force the Seattle Police Department to reopen the investigation.

Using the important new testimony from the former police chief Norm Stamper and Cyril Wecht's compelling and credible findings, I intend to soon hold a press conference outside Seattle Police Headquarters with the family of one of the copycat suicide victims whose son took his own life, leaving a note that he had done it "for Kurt."

The parents — ideally flanked by both myself and Norm Stamper — will use the occasion to announce that they are launching a civil suit to compel the Seattle Police to reopen the investigation for the sake of the 68 families whose children may have committed suicide under the mistaken impression that their hero had done so, signalling to a generation for whom he was the voice that their lives were no longer worth living. Legal experts have concluded that the new evidence and the former police chief's admission may or may not result in a murder verdict but will almost certainly force the department to change their findings from suicide to "undetermined."

One of the most puzzling aspects connected to this long drawn investigation is how key people connected to Courtney keep ending up dead. First there was the "accidental death" of medical examiner Nikolas Hartshorne who admitted to me when I interviewed him at his office back in 1995 that he had dated Courtney in the past. He didn't try to hide his conflict of interest. He admitted in an ideal world someone else would have been the person conducting the autopsy on Kurt. "Perhaps it is a bit weird," he told me. When I pressed him if he was still close to Courtney, he replied "yes, we are very close. But I really don't see anything wrong with it."

Hartshorne was born September 14, 1963 in Manchester, Great Manchester, England. He died on August 6, 2002 in Lauterbrunnen, Bern, Switzerland in a BASE jumping accident. He jumped off a cliff known as "The Nose". Hartshorne had been a very skilled and experienced BASE jumper for many years. In an interview with one of his former best friends in mid 2022, I learned that Harshorne's death most likely was not an accident. It might have been suicide.

"Nik was one of the most experienced BASE jumpers in the world," the friend said. "There's no way it was an accident. I know for a fact how much Nik was tormented all those years by Kurt's death and his conflict of interest. He became depressed and was not the same outgoing, fun loving person I knew way back in the late eighties and early nineties. After Kurt died he started following Tom Grant's website and serious allegations against Courtney. When your first book (Who Killed Kurt Cobain) was published he started to backtrack on his verdict. He told me several times he thought he might have been duped by Courtney to cover up Kurt's death. Seemingly, he started to change his attitude and his entire personality. I barely recognized him the last time I saw him, which was for tea a few weeks before he died. I really believe he couldn't cope with his involvement and guilt in Kurt's death any longer and decided to leave this world. He was a consummate professional and the fact he realized he might have made a huge error on his verdict about Kurt's death haunted him like a passion. He was never able to live with himself again and never got over it."

I decided to follow up further and interview another person close to Hartshorne, a former colleague who to this day believes his former friend's death was not accidental.

"No way," she told me. "Nik was one of the best

jumpers in the world. I believe someone tampered with his jump and wanted him dead. Even though he seemed to act strange in the years before he died, I don't think he would have taken his own life. Nik loved life way too much. He was a man of passion who always said he wanted to live till a hundred and ten."

Furthermore, the colleague revealed to me Hartshorne told her on at least two occasions he feared for his life, that someone might be trying to kill him in order to silence him.

"He knew way too much about the Cobain file and was far too connected to it," she said. "He even had posters of Kurt hanging in his office. I think he got in over his head involved in the case and couldn't cope with the fact he might have made a huge professional error. He knew way too much and when someone knows too much in a possible murder cover up they easily become the next target. And that's what I believe happened here. I think someone paid to have him taken out."

The next key person to die mysteriously connected to the case was El Duce, former lead singer and drummer of the heavy metal band The Mentors who went on record to describe how Courtney Love offered him $50,000 "to blow Kurt's head off". Duce, whose real name was Eldon Wayne Hoke, died on April 19, 1997, one day after his final gig. Interestingly, it happened eight days after filming an interview with British documentary filmmaker Nick Broomfield for the cult classic Kurt

& Courtney film. I worked as a consultant on the film and discovered Hoke's incredible allegations to be more concerning than outrageous, as many media depicted. He told Broomfield that Courtney offered him 50k to "whack" Cobain and that someone named "Allen" took the offer. The person he referred to was porn metal singer Allen Wrench, whom I interviewed at length for the film I directed The Cobain Case. Wrench corroborated everything Hoke said but added further fire, boasting he was the one who ended up pulling the trigger on Kurt. Wrench told his story with conviction. However, years later I met a former bandmate of Wrench at an L.A. heavy metal concert who would contradict his story. He told me, "Allen was a guy who would do anything for publicity, anything to get his name out there. He would lie a lot. And in this case I for one believe he made it all up just to shock people. I don't think he had any involvement in Kurt's death."

Meanwhile, Hoke passed a polygraph with flying colors administered by one of the world's leading polygraph examiners, Ed Gelb, a few days before he died. Ironically, it was Gelb who administered the polygraph to OJ Simpson when he was in jail on first degree murder charges which OJ failed miserably. Al Jorgenson, of the industrial band Ministry, claimed that El Duce was killed by the train when some groupies yelled out his name on the other side of the tracks and as Duce tried to cross the tracks to meet them his toes got stuck in the track. The tragic event happened in Riverside, California where Duce resided. A police investigator in Riverside didn't buy Jorgenson's theory. "Nothing adds up," he told me back in 2016. "I believe a proper investigation was never done into Hoke's death. I've never heard of someone's toe getting caught in the tracks and then getting hit by an oncoming train. I think someone got him piss drunk on purpose and led him to the tracks so he would get killed. Weeks later, I learned about how he gave the interview in the film and things started to become more clear. I think someone wanted to stop him talking any further and had him set up to be taken out."

Another person close to the case who died suspiciously and whose family to this day claims he was murdered was Courtney Love's long time gumshoe private investigator Jack Palladino. Palladino, whose client list included Bill Clinton, convicted sex offender Harvey Weinstein, corporate whistleblowers and Hollywood's elite stars and producers, died February 1, 2021 outside his home in San Francisco. Palladino was attacked outside his Haight-Ashbury Victorian home and suffered a severe brain injury resulting from a drive-by attempt to rob a new camera he had stepped outside to try out. A car pulled up and a man fought Palladino for it. As the suspect grabbed the camera, Palladino fell hard on the pavement, hitting his head which caused a traumatic head injury. Incredibly, Palladino was able to snap images of the suspects before hitting his head which turned out to be the key evidence in arresting the two prime suspects.

Police used the photos to track down and arrest the men. "He helped solve his own murder," Palladino's attorney Mel Honowitz said.

The key question remains is why anyone would want to hurt Palladino, who was at the end of his career and on the road to a nice retirement. Certainly, if one of his old clients was behind Palladino's death the only prime suspect would be none other than Courtney Love. Why? I met with Palladino several times over the years - first when he trespassed in my backyard in Montreal and offered to buy me dinner anywhere I wanted to get more information on my investigation. I met him again a year later in the mid nineties when I embarked on a cross country lecture tour about Cobain's death. Palladino showed up to the Toronto show at the Opera House and jumped on stage to try to defend Courtney. He started to debate me before he got booed offstage. He told the Toronto audience, "Ian's lying, there's no book and will never be a book". The fact Jack is, there was not one book, but two books (now three) and multiple films. I told Palladino in front of the jam-packed Toronto crowd that I won't back down until justice in Kurt's case is served.

Palladino tried to stop both books from being published. For the second book, a day before publication he showed up to Simon&Schuster's office on 6th Ave., in Manhattan. The publisher called me, telling me Palladino's in the lobby trying to stop the book. I asked what they intended to do. "We're watching him on security cameras. In fact, we're laughing quite hard. He's a fool. In another fifteen minutes we'll have security throw him out on the street."

The truth of the matter is that Jack and I actually got along quite well. He told me several times, "Ian, I'm only doing my job. I actually think you're a nice, honest guy."

At dinner, he told me to take my time. I asked him why. He responded, "because I'm getting paid very well to have dinner with you. Please don't rush."

As for the case, he admitted to me his client wasn't exactly "the most normal client he ever took on. Certainly, Courtney is a bit out of control. But that doesn't mean she murdered her husband," he said. I pressed Jack further, asking him if he knew 100 percent Courtney had nothing to do with Kurt's murder. "No," he quickly replied. "There's no way in hell I can be sure of that. And that's not my job. In life, you never know."

According to multiple sources, as the years progressed Palladino distanced himself from Courtney. As his famed client kept getting into more trouble with the law and drugs Palladino privately started to question the veracity of his client. "He thought she was a bit of a loose cannon," a longtime friend of Palladino said back in 2014. "In fact, I know for a fact he questions Courtney's true role in Kurt's death. Jack got tired of defending Courtney because she kept getting into big trouble over the years. He didn't want his own reputation to get smeared forever by defending her. He thought where there's smoke there's fire and that Courtney wasn't completely upfront with him about the events surrounding Kurt's death. He really didn't want to be a part of the case anymore, but he sort of had no choice. I really don't think he was convinced his client was telling the complete truth. But then again, that's not his job. People hire him, and he has to do what they ask of him. That's the way it works."

Another former associate of the famed private investigator said Palladino once hinted to him that when he retired he planned to spill the beans about the Cobain file and urge authorities to do a proper investigation. "Jack was a man of honor, he never did anything illegal," the associate who asked to be referred to as "Joe" said. "He certainly had concerns about Kurt's death and wanted to get to the bottom of it. He once hinted that if the case was reopened he'd have no choice but to cooperate with Seattle police privately and turn over his notes to them. But he said he'd only do it if they were serious about doing a proper investigation. He was really put in an innocuous position on that file."

Almost two years to the day Palladino died, the charges against the suspects in his death were dropped after a witness admitted he never saw one of the men in the passengers seat attempt to steal Palladino's camera through the car window. Furthermore, the suspect's DNA left no traces on the camera. Palladino's family were left appalled by the dismissal. Circumstantial evidence, they claimed, clearly demonstrated that the men tried to steal Palladino's camera, which caused his death. Police were unable, however, to track down video of Palladino making contact with the men.

"There's no question in our minds, and it's our opinion the two defendants were in fact the killers of Jack Palladino," Palladino's lawyer Mel Honowitz exclaimed. "We understood the decision by the district attorney. We don't necessarily agree with it."

Both suspects were released from a San Francisco jail.

"The whole thing is very odd," "Joe" said. "For some reason I don't think the police took Jack's death too seriously. It's clear he was murdered. Why would they dismiss it on such weak grounds? I think there's much more to this and someone was behind the men attacking Jack. We will never find out unless a proper investigation is done. But in my mind, someone out there along with the suspects are breathing a huge sigh of relief that they didn't get caught."

Another longtime friend of Palladino, who

asked for anonymity, summed it up best. "Jack was a wonderful person, a legend with a big heart. There's no way in my mind that his death was not a murder. Jack had great balance and was sturdy. There's no way he fell unless he was taken out. The question is why? Why would someone attack him as he was finally starting to embrace retirement? I don't think it was to get his new camera. It wouldn't be worth it. I think someone might have paid these men a nice price to take out poor Jack. He will be missed forever by his close friends and colleagues."

There's no timeline that exists for when it's ok to talk negatively about someone after they die. Social media is swamped with capital "RIP" letters and heart emojis after someone famous dies. In Courtney Love's father's case, critics didn't waste any time highlighting his faults and failures, even if other people who knew him were mourning. These days, even the most incredible person in the world could die and some people would still go out of their way to stomp on their virtual grave. More than enough time, however, has passed to allow for a closer examination of Courtney Love's enigmatic father.

Hank Harrison, Courtney biological and most controversial dad, passed away of heart failure on January 22, 2022. With a legacy like his - manager of Phil Lesh's band, The Warlocks, which became the Grateful Dead and having written two bestselling books about the band - one would think at least every major music magazine would cover his death, let alone every daily newspaper. Interestingly, not even a small blurb or mention anywhere except in a few newspapers, including the local paper The Galt Herald in the small California town where Harrison lived.

Harrison's most recent tome before he died was in 2017, "Love Kills: The Assassination of Kurt Cobain". The book received almost no publicity in the mainstream media, similar to his death which was announced to little pity parties on social media by his wife of 42 years, Catriona Watson.

For years the egocentric Harrison told anyone who would listen how Courtney was behind Kurt's death, drawing on all the information made available to Tom Grant. Harrison really knew nothing about any of the details of the case, having been estranged from Courtney most her life since he got divorced from Courtney's mother Linda in 1969. In turn, Courtney claimed her father was nothing else but a loose cannon, having given her LSD when she was just a toddler. She also admitted that they briefly lived together in Ireland. Harrison claimed that they lived together in Irleand for seven months and "got along amazing". Courtney, however, told a different story. She said she only stayed with her dad for a few days because he was physically violent against her and "beat me up badly". It's obvious the apple doesn't fall too far from the tree in this dysfunctional family. Both Harrison and Courtney have been proven to be pathological liars. The two hadn't seen each other since 1993, when Harrison drove Courtney to play at her band's Hole concert in the Bay area. Harrison said he didn't stay for the show. Unfortunately, Harrison never realized his one erstwhile dream - to meet his granddaughter, Frances Bean Cobain. Also, he never met his son-in-law, Kurt.

"The one thing I want to do in my life is to meet my granddaughter," Harrison told me back in 1995, when I first met him at his California ranch, that seemed to have more wild pitbulls than horses on its land. "If Courtney decides to call me, of course I would do whatever I had to to support her and get her out of this mess. She's still my daughter. We're so alike, that's why we don't get along. We have the same crazy, high IQ DNA. No matter what she did she's my blood. All she needs to do is pick up the phone and I would be there for her."

I found it strange how Hank on one hand openly accused his daughter of murder and on the other wanted reconciliation with her. I pressed him further, and was shocked by how far a father of a daughter can go.

"Courtney's a complete psychopath," he told me. "Kurt wanted a divorce and that's why she had him killed. If he wasn't killed her bank Hole would have never broken out the way it did. Anybody who ever gets in Courtney's way should beware. She will do anything to save her own skin."

I met Hank at least a couple more times over the years, in Canada on a multi-media tour about the mysterious events surrounding Kurt's death and also at the syndicated Maury Pauvich Show in New York, in which I got completely taken aback backstage when he boasted to me how much money he stood to make by promoting the murder theory. Moreover, he finally admitted he knew nothing about the case except what he had read from Tom Grant or from the book I coauthored with Max Wallace, Who Killed Kurt Cobain.

"This is my one chance to make a fortune," he told me. "I will publish my own book and it will sell millions because I'm Courtney's father. I'm the one person who people will take seriously about this because I'm Courtney's father. I'm the only person who know who Courtney really is and psychopath personality she has. Poor Kurt didn't know what he was really getting into when he married my crazy daughter."

That was enough for me. Originally, I liked Hank but to hear someone openly accuse his own daughter of murder disgusted me. Clearly, as he admitted, he had ulterior motives which would only be detrimental to the case and knock down the hard evidence everyone else was working diligently to expose to help get Kurt's case reopened.

Still, without really knowing anything about Kurt's death, Harrison was able to concoct the most powerful and incriminating line related to the case. Police examiners concluded shotgun that killed Kurt had no latent fingerprints on it. Harrison said: "Dead men don't wipe their own prints."

Still, no matter how disconnected and sleazy

Harrison appeared to be related to Kurt's case, it remains a huge enigma why music publications who forever covered anything connected to Courtney, like Rolling Stone or Spin, never covered his death. Who was behind muzzling these mainstay publications? In a fair media era, Harrison's death would have merited at least a couple paragraphs about what he accomplished with The Grateful Dead, his books and the fact that he openly accused his famous rock icon daughter of murder.

Two other key people in Seattle during that time connected to or Courtney also died mysteriously. On June 16, 1994, Hole bassist Kristen Pfaff was found dead in the bathtub of her Seattle apartment. Again, it was the controversial medical examiner, Nikolas Hartshorne, who ruled Kristen's death a suicide. Hawthorne concluded it was a "classic suicide", and went out of his way for some reason to say it was much like Kurt's "suicide". Suspiciously, there was no toxicology test conducted. If Kristen would have have overdosed on drugs, like Hartshorne said, why wouldn't he have ordered a toxicology? Was Hartshorne again trying to cover up for his ex-girlfriend Courtney Love? Furthermore, the autopsy report was never released to the public - it's been almost 30 years since she passed.

At the time of her death, Kristen was leaving Courtney, just like Kurt. She told Courtney she was leaving Hole and was heading back to Minneapolis to reunite with her old band, Janitor Joe. She had a packed Uhaul outside her apartment and was ready to leave with her friend Paul Erickson. The last person to see Kristen alive was her longtime lover, Hole guitarist Eric Erlandson. Erlandson would later admit his guilt about Kristen's death. "I admit, I made some stupid mistakes with some people, and people are dead because of my stupid mistakes."

I interviewed several people in Kristen's immediate family following her death. Her mother Janet and brother Jason stressed to me how Kristen had gone to rehab and was clean when she died. They described to me how much she feared Courtney and was excited to leave Seattle to make a new start.

Clearly, Courtney showed motive to taking out Kristen. She became obsessed with the idea that Kurt was cheating on her with another woman. She labeled Kristen as a prime suspect. On April 1, 1994, a few days before Kurt died, Kurt purchased to airline tickets for him and another woman. Courtney told people in her inner circle she suspected the "mystery woman" might have been none other than Kristen. Courtney accused Kristen multiple times of trying to steal Kurt, an accusation Kristen vehemently denied, saying they were "just good friends".

Perhaps the smoking gun in Kristen's death was the odd discovery by her mother Janet. When Janet received Kristen's belongings after she died she noticed several pages from Kristen's diary had been torn out. The missing entries were the entries during the week when Kurt went missing from a

L.A. drug rehab center to the day his body was found. Why would someone have torn out these pages? Did Kristen write something that would have incriminated someone linked to Kurt's death? Clearly, nobody in Kristen's family believes she died of an overdose. They believe she knew too much and was taken out to be silenced forever.

Finally, another highly suspicious death was that of Detective Antonio Terry, a narcotics detective for the Seattle Police Department who was murdered in a very strange shooting incident a couple of months after Kurt died. Terry became the first Seattle police officer killed on duty in more than nine years. He had left work and was on his way home when pulled over to investigate a stalled vehicle. Terry was then shot and killed.

Terry had been close to Courtney Love for years. The often spoke on the phone. Tom Grant taped them several times. Courtney claimed she was close to Terry because she was helping him get local drug dealers busted. Why in the world would a heavy drug user like Courtney help Seattle police bust local drug dealers? It made no sense. Once source in the Seattle police department admitted to me, Courtney used Detective Terry to protect herself from the law.

"Essentially Courtney Love got immunity from Seattle police because she became a drug informant," the source said. "That's why she was proven to above the law in Seattle up until this day. The written rule was not to mess with Courtney. She knew a lot about the Seattle drug and crime scene and became a big informant over the years giving leads to the cops."

The source added that Terry went out of his way to cover up records and documents to protect Courtney.

"They were very, very close," the source said. "I later found out from people who were close to Terry that he shredded documents to help protect Courtney. Courtney would have most likely gotten in trouble with law were it not for Terry covering up for her."

There was a plethora of drug overdose deaths in Seattle in the nineties. That might be the simplest and best explanation why Seattle police thought Kurt Cobain was just another junkie in the area taking his own life. Let's face it, Kurt Cobain was the perfect candidate to take his own life, having written about suicide and being no stranger to heroin and guns. However, as top forensic experts quoted in this book point out, the evidence that Kurt was murdered is overwhelming, including: (I will not go into too much detail here because it's all outlined in the first too books I coauthored).

The Suicide Note. Experts have claimed for years that the note was about Kurt planning to leave the music business, not life. However, the last five lines - the only section of the note that discusses suicide - were in someone else's handwriting. Top handwriting experts that analyzed the note note concur that the bottom five lines was written by someone trying to copy Kurt's handwriting.

Interestingly, a "practice sheet" was found in Courtney's handbag with the form and shape of letter that actually almost match perfectly letters and form in the last five lines. Many experts have concluded it wasn't a suicide note at all but the last five lines were added to make it look like one. "I've examined hundreds of suicide notes over the years," one leading German handwriting expert told me. "This case is one of the most blatant instances of the note being tampered with. The last five lines were written by someone else, not Kurt."

Furthermore, as detailed in my previous books, the amount of heroin in Kurt's system was too high for any human being to remain conscious more than a couple of seconds. It was 70 times the lethal dose for the average person and three times the lethal dose for the most severe junkie. As experts have explained already in this book, it would be impossible for anyone to inject the heroin, remove the syringe, place it back in his box, roll down his sleeve, pick up a shotgun and then blow his head off. There's no precedent of anyone ever doing such a thing. It's impossible, that according to multiple forensic experts who have examined Kurt's case over the years.

While the peak of junkies in Seattle taking their own lives peaked in the nineties, it has significantly declined there in recent years. Today, it's much easier to solve case similar to Kurt's with the advent of genetic approaches to tracking offenders and the higher prospect of capture that deters potential killers from acting out.

When Kurt's body was found by an electrician

installing a security system he had gone missing for six days. His body was found in the greenhouse above the garage of his Lake Washington home. Police claimed his body had been lying there for two and a half days and that a high concentration of heroin and traces of Valium were found in his bloodstream. The details of his journey back to Seattle from Los Angeles were murky, with many people speculating but not giving hard core proof on the exact timeline and his exact whereabouts. For years, I've tried to track it down to a tee but must admit there remains to this day many questions. However, I was able to track down several people with key information, including one brave man who was willing to give me key information. He believes Kurt was running in fear for his life and that there's no other explanation to his death other than "murder".

The never-before-revealed slam dunk that clearly demonstrates that Kurt was afraid for his life comes from a man who claims he spoke to Kurt the same day Kurt escaped from an L.A. drug rehab center days before he was found dead. The man, who is of Croatian descent and now lives back in its capital city Zagreb, contacted me through a Bulgarian friend in the summer of 2022, when I was on tour with my band. (For years I've been a professional sax player, playing small clubs and festivals). "Franjo" detailed to me how he smoked a cigarette with Kurt that same day and got a lot of information out of him in their five minute encounter. "I used to wash dishes in L.A. and one day across the street at a gas station from where I worked I noticed a man who I thought was my hero, Kurt Cobain," "Franjo" said. "I rushed across the street and asked him if he was Kurt Cobain. He replied yes. He asked me for a cigarette. I obliged. We started talking about music and left-handed guitars ("Franjo" also played guitar and was like Kurt played left) and talked briefly about Nirvana. Kurt seemed completely coherent but seemed to be in a rush.

"I asked him where he was heading, he replied "far, far away. Somewhere calm and safe for me and my daughter." "Franjo" who had a baby son told Kurt how the most wonderful thing in life was being a dad and that nothing else mattered. Kurt, "Franjo" said nodded in agreement. Kurt then left and "Franjo" returned from his break back to his dishwashing job.

The fact that "Franjo" recalled Kurt being so cool headed, calm but looking for safety describes it all to anyone doubting the murder theory.

"It took me years to realize how much danger Kurt was in," "Franjo" admitted. "That's why I finally contacted you. It was very clear that Kurt had no intention of taking his own life but rather was worried for his safety. He knew someone was trying to hurt him. It's too bad he was in such a hurry. Maybe I could have got him to tell me who he was running from. To this day I know he was murdered. Having studied all the evidence, and having met

Kurt shortly before he died, it's clear police got this case wrong. Why would anyone who was so proud to be a father want to die blowing his head off and living that grisly image imprinted forever in the mind of the most precious person in his life - Frances. If Kurt wanted to die he could have easily just overdosed and said goodbye in a peaceful way. There's no way in a million years the man I briefly met wanted to die. All he wanted was to be in a safe, quiet place for him and Frances. Nothing was ever more clear than that to me in my entire life."

No matter how the amazingly talented musician Kurt Cobain was killed, the person who finally has to step up and clear her name is Kurt's widow Courtney Love. By all accounts, most likely Courtney was involved in a murder conspiracy. Why would any grieving widow do everything in her powers all these years to make the murder allegations go away. It's almost the same as O.J. saying he would hunt down Nicole and Ron's killers after he was acquitted in that botched L.A. trial.

I'm willing to give Courtney a chance to finally clear her name by accepting my offer to take a polygraph test in Los Angeles with one of the world's leading polygraph examiners. I will gladly pay for the test at her convenience.

Still, if Courtney passes the test I will conclude unwaveringly that the voice of a generation was murdered and that it's time to reopen the case, do a proper investigation and bring to justice those involved. The world owes it to the voice of a generation, Kurt Cobain, to get to the bottom of how he really died and seek justice for him. Kurt can never be replaced but there's no doubt how he would want the hundreds of copycat suicides to stop. He would also want justice and for those who killed him to finally be held accountable.

Another person who I challenge to take a polygraph is Michael "Cali Dewitt, long suspected in being involved in Kurt's death. Most believer in the murder theory believe that Cali was the one who murdered Kurt at Courtney's request. Again, it was Courtney who gave Cali $30,000 to go to rehab and was long rumored to have an affair with Courtney. I will reserve judgment on Cali's role until he takes a polygraph. If he passes, I will make sure to post everywhere in the world that he is innocent.

Message To Courtney Love: Courtney, lets finally get to the bottom of this and seek justice for your husband. I prove it was scientifically impossible for Kurt to have committed suicide. If you notice, in this book I just lay out the new evidence and go out of my way not to convict you. The ball is now in your court. Please accept my offer to take the polygraph. And if you pass, I will pay for a billboard in Times Square proclaiming your innocence. Then, lets band together to set up a huge manhunt to finally hold the person or people accountable for killing Kurt. This book makes it 100 percent clear Kurt was murdered. Any concerned spouse would accept this offer, Courtney. It's fair and it's time to seek justice for Kurt! You can accept the offer by sending me a DM to me on Twitter @ianundercover

ACKNOWLEDGEMENT

To all the brave people who have joined me, including Tom Grant, Max Wallace, Leland Cobain and countless others, in going on record to demand the Cobain Case be reopened in order for a proper investigation to be conducted into how the legendary leader of Nirvana really died.

ABOUT THE AUTHOR

Ian Halperin

#1 NY Times bestselling author Ian Halperin is widely known as one of the top non-fiction authors of his generation. He has written many bestselling books which have been translated all over the world. Halperin is also an award-winning film director and professional saxophone player. Halperin is a regular guest and contributor to: NBC, CBS, ABC, CNN, Fox Billboard, London Daily Mail, and Sirius XM.

CONTROVERSY: SEX, LIES AND DIRTY MONEY BY THE WORLD'S POWERFUL ELITE

A no-holds barred investigation by No. 1 NY Times bestselling author Ian Halperin. It offers the most extensive journey ever into incredible, tumultuous and shadowy lives of the world's most famous. CONTROVERSY will go down as the mother, definitive journalistic work about the abuse of power and celebrity by the world's rich and famous.

Case Closed: The Cobain Murder: The Killing And Cover Up Of Kurt Cobain

A riveting investigation proving that rock icon Kurt Cobain was murdered.

Controversy: (Prince Andrew And

Jeffrey Epstein)

An incredible look at the real relationship between sociopath Jeffrey Epstein and Prince Andrew. Halperin was the only person to every interview sociopath Epstein at length.

Keeping Secrets: Undercover In The Hollywood Closet

In his new book Inside the Hollywood Closet, Ian Halperin — author of the number one New York Times-bestseller Unmasked — unveils in astonishing detail the startling findings of his decade-long investigation that has seen him join a celebrity cult, apply for a job as an L.A. escort, ride through the Hollywood Hills with a drug dealer to the stars, and participate in a weekly show business poker game known as the Queers of the Round Table. Along the way, he unveils the workings of an industry heavily invested in maintaining an illusion that bears no semblance to reality and which can't afford to allow the public to know how deeply homosexuality is ingrained in Hollywood and the music business. His riveting exposé — which, among other things, sees him infiltrate the Church of Scientology posing as a gay actor seeking a "cure" — spotlights the devastating emotional toll the industry's self-imposed closet takes on hundreds of celebrities and the staggering effort to maintain the code of silence with billions of dollars at stake

Who Killed The Beatles?: All You Need Is Love - Linda, Mccartney, Yoko Ono And The Breakup That Shook The World

This captivating exploration exposes the heartbreaking never-before-revealed secrets of who really was behind the breakup of The Fab Four.Hundreds of books have been written about the world's most famous rock band. Writers have delved into every conceivable facet of their history, from their hard-scrabble Liverpool origins to the advent of Beatlemania and beyond. But award-winning investigative journalist Ian Halperin — whose acclaimed books about Kurt Cobain, Michael Jackson and Whitney Houston have gained him a reputation as a music chronicler with a difference — has pieced together one of the few chapters of Beatles history that has never been told. In the process, he discovered a remarkable story that explodes a number of myths about the Beatles and sheds a fascinating new light on the complicated history of John and Paul both before and after the group's 1970 breakup. It is a chapter of the group's history that has eluded most previous chroniclers because the Beatles' story has always been told by music journalists who have mostly peddled the mythology that the Beatles broke up over creative or personal differences. However, as Halperin discovered by interviewing dozens of key figures associated with the band and its music company, Apple Corps, there was one factor above all that came between the once inseparable boyhood mates and eventually led to the demise of the most popular rock group of all time.

Michael Jackson - Unmasked Ii: Dismantling The Neverland Accusations

Unmasked II, #1 NY Times bestselling author Ian Halperin examines shocking allegations made by two former Jackson associates - Wade Robson and James Safechuck - made in the documentary film Finding Neverland that awakened a sleep ghost from a decade-long slumber. The film appeared once and for all to lay to rest any doubt - a once beloved icon was in fact a monster.

Once again child molestation allegations were at the center. However, this time The King of Pop was not here to defend himself. Both men, however, claimed that they were not interested in money and had only come forward to embolden other abuse victims to speak out. It is these words that set off alarm bells for author Halperin and reminded him of the previous Jackson accusers whose dubious claims were shown to have almost certainly been motivated by money all along. Deciding to dig deeper into the court records, Halperin discovered some very telling evidence that appeared to contradict the men's claims of selflessness.

Jackson had always claimed that he liked to be around young boys because he had been deprived of a normal childhood. His behavior, therefore, was akin to the kind of sleepovers and play dates that most children participate in during their childhood. Halperin concludes that, although the singer's pattern of behavior was undeniably creepy, the testimony of dozens of eyewitnesses corroborate Jackson's innocence. Along with scores of contradictions and inconsistencies elsewhere in their stories, it suggests that Robson and Safechuck mostly told the truth about their encounters with Jackson. That is why they came off so convincingly on camera. But when they ran into financial difficulties, they almost certainly added the molestation allegations in order to cash in from the estate.

And, although Unmasked II largely exonerates Jackson from the accusations that threaten to erase his legacy, it provides a warts-and-all perspective on Jackson's life and personality and blames his arrogance rather than naiveté for ignoring the years of warnings from friends and family about his relationships with children and the public optics.

Halperin reveals the untold truths about the scurrilous accusations agains Jackson, uncovering a plethora of new evidence that the child molestation allegations against him were part of a huge cash grab to extract millions of dollars from the late superstar's estate.

AFTERWORD

The ball is now in Courtney Love's court. If she agrees to take the polygraph exam, clearly she's taking a step in the right direction to exonerate herself from the serious allegations against her all these years. If she refuses - enough said!

EPILOGUE

The last word goes to my longtime source in the Seattle police department who wants the world to know that he's optimistic the Cobain case will be reopened sooner than later. He told me he wants all of Kurt's fans to never lose HOPE.

The longtime law enforcement official was brave enough to give me this quote in HOPE of seeking justice.

"In life we need to seek justice for those who have been hurt," he told me. "Courage and practical wisdom are the key virtues of justice. After studying extensively every fact, document and timeline in Kurt Cobain's case I conclude without an iota of doubt that this case was a complete cover up and that the police got it completely wrong. The facts cannot be more clear. It's time to seek justice amidst all the chaos and document the individuals implicated in the murder of Kurt Cobain. I urge my colleagues in Seattle to please be brave and not remain silent. The painful truths in this enigmatic case unsettle not only our foes but also our friends and, most especially, ourselves. Kurt Cobain's death was never properly investigated. It's time to find out why, and time to get to the bottom of a case that, based on all the forensic evidence, should have never been ruled a suicide"

*Kurt's suicide note

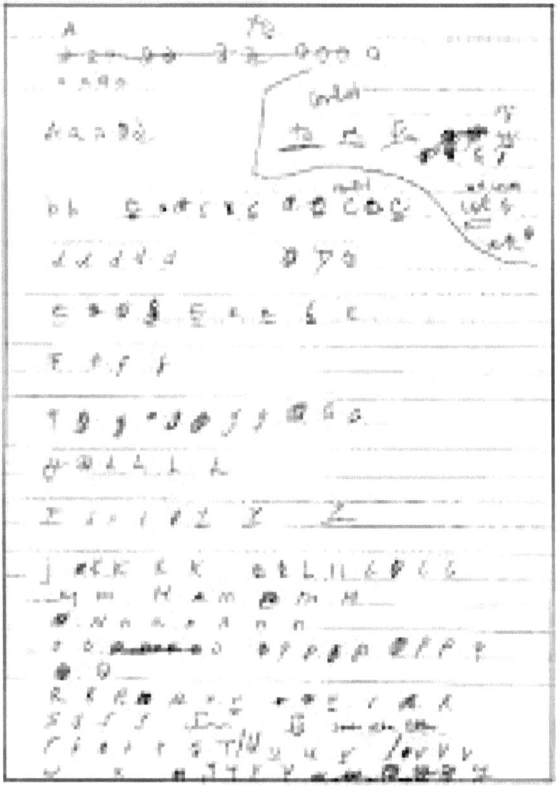

*Handwriting Practice Found In Courtney Love's Backpack

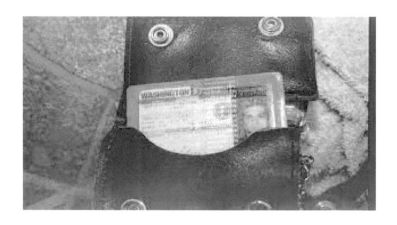

*Photos Taken at Scene of Kurt's Death

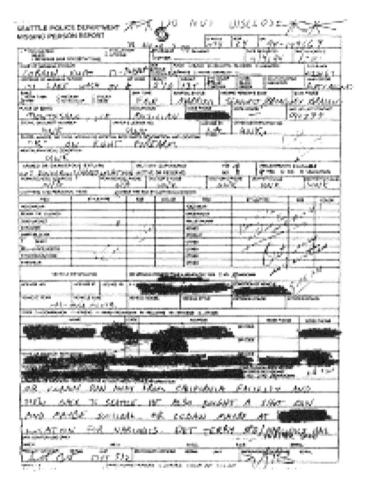

*Missing Persons Report

*Cobain Death Certificate was labeled suicide before Dr. Hartshorne had the results of the toxicology report.

INSURANCE COMPANY LETTER

Insurance Company Name	Name: ALLEN DRAKER, TRUSTEE* and KURT D. COBAIN
Newton Insurance Agency	Policy Number:
Address	Property:
12729 NE 20th Street, #12	XX Home ☐ Auto ☐ Boat ☐ Other
	Address Of Description:
Bellevue, WA 98005	171 LAKE WASH. BLVD. EAST
City	
John B. Shay	SEATTLE, WA 98112
Date	
JANUARY 21, 1994	LOAN # 047384-7

Gentlemen:

I have this date executed a Mortgage/Deed of Trust/Builder's & Mechanic's Lien Contract/Deed to Secure Debt or Promissory Note/Promissory Note and Security Agreement with respect to the above-referenced property to:

CHASE MANHATTAN PERSONAL FINANCIAL SERVICES, INC. and/or its successors & assigns
Office Name

P.O. BOX 30166
Address

TAMPA, FL 33630

as collateral for acceptable consideration.

Kindly issue to Chase, at its address above, a short form copy of said policy showing the amount of coverage of my property, date of policy, and endorsement naming the above named office as:
XX First loss payee/Mortgagee, or ☐ Loss Payee.
If the coverage under my homeowner's policy is less than $1,159,750.00/REPLACEMENT COST CLAUSE
_____, which is the balance of my outstanding liens or the structural value of my property, please increase the coverage to this amount and bill me for the additional premium.

Flood Insurance: ☐ check if applicable

The above property is located in a flood prone area. Kindly issue a lender's loss payee endorsement for flood coverage in the amount of $ N/A   which is the amount of my outstanding liens or the maximum amount available under the National Flood Insurance Program.

Comments:
*ALLEN DRAKER, TRUSTEE FOR THE 171 LAKE WASHINGTON BOULEVARD EAST TRUST
AGREEMENT DATED JANUARY 19, 1994

PLEASE REFERENCE ABOVE LOAN NUMBER ON ALL FUTURE CORRESPONDENCE

Customer Signature, Trustee 1-21-94
ALLEN DRAKER, TRUSTEE*

Customer Signature 1-21-94
KURT D. COBAIN

Customer Signature   Date

Customer Signature   Date

*Cobain homeowner insurance policy signed less than three months before his death.

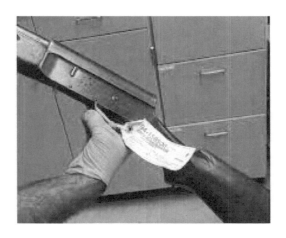

*Remington Model 11 20-gauge shotgun found at scene of Kurt's death.

☐ INCIDENT		INCIDENT NUMBER
☐ INCIDENT AND ARREST		94-123078
☐ ARREST ONLY		

☐ DO NOT DISCLOSE   ☐ NOT DISCOVERED   ☐ DISCLOSE

I HEREBY DECLARE THE FACTS HEREIN REPORTED BY ME ARE TRUE AND CORRECT. I UNDERSTAND
THAT BY FILING A FALSE REPORT, I MAY BE SUBJECT TO CRIMINAL PROSECUTION.

☐ HAZARD TO OFFICER
☐ DOMESTIC VIOLENCE

INCIDENT CLASSIFICATION
V.P.A. DISTURBANCE

TOOL/WEAPON USED

METHOD OF TOOL/WEAPON USE

LOCATION	FIRM NAME		CENSUS	BEAT
	N/A		078	C4

TYPE OF PREMISE (FOR VEHICLES STATE TYPE AND WHERE PARKED)

POINT OF ENTRY

DATE/TIME REPORTED		DAY OF WEEK	DATE/TIME OCCURRED			DAY OF WEEK
03-18-94	1810	FRI	03-18-94		1810	FRI

☐ EVIDENCE SUBMITTED   ☐ FINGERPRINT SEARCH MADE   ☐ FINGERPRINTS FOUND   ☐ LAB EXAM REQUESTED

INJURED   HAS USABLE TESTIMONY   DO NOT DISCLOSE

CODE	C PERSON REPORTING (COMPLAINANT) V VICTIM W WITNESS						
C	NAME (LAST, FIRST, MIDDLE)			RACE/SEX/D.O.B. W/F/		HOME PHONE	HOURS
	ADDRESS		ZIP CODE 98122	OCCUPATION (OPTIONAL)		WORK PHONE	HOURS
W	NAME (LAST, FIRST, MIDDLE)			RACE/SEX/D.O.B. (OPTIONAL) U/N/		HOME PHONE	HOURS
	ADDRESS		ZIP CODE 98122	OCCUPATION (OPTIONAL)		WORK PHONE	HOURS

NAME (LAST, FIRST, MIDDLE) COBAIN, KURT D	RACE/SEX/D.O.B. W/M/ 02-20-67	HEIGHT 5-08	WEIGHT 140	HAIR BLD	EYES BLUE	SKIN TONE FAIR	BUILD SLM
ADDRESS 171 LAKE WASHINGTON BLVD E.	HOME PHONE	WORK PHONE	WORK HOURS	OCCUPATION		EMPLOYER/SCHOOL	

CLOTHING, SCARS, MARKS, TATTOOS, PECULIARITIES, A.K.A.
BLUE SHIRT, BLUE JEANS, WHITE TENNIS SHOES

W.C.T. NO.   CHARGE DETAILS (INCLUDE ORDINANCE OR R.C.W. NUMBER AND CHARGE NARRATIVE.)

INTERVIEWED AND RELEASED

☐ 800×800 ☐ Y&G   ☐ &G×.®
☐ GT®   ☐ K.G.L. #   ☐ K.G.L. ®

☐ ADDITIONAL PROPERTY (PROPERTY FORM 5.27.1 MUST BE ATTACHED)   ☐ NOTHING TAKEN   ☐ UNKNOWN AT TIME OF REPORT   ☐ VICTIM FOLLOW-UP LEFT

ARTICLE TYPE	BRAND NAME	VALUE
☐ STOLEN SERIAL NUMBER	OWNER APPLIED NUMBER	MODEL NUMBER
☐ RECOVERED		

COLOR, SIZE, DESCRIPTION, CALIBER, BARREL LENGTH ETC.

1. ADDITIONAL PERSONS - CODE, NAME, RACE, SEX, D.O.B., ADDRESS, INJURY,
   HOSPITALIZATION, HOME AND WORK PHONES, HOURS, AND IF DISCLOSURE OF NAME
   IS PERMITTED.
2. ADDITIONAL SUSPECTS - DETAIL INFORMATION IN SAME ORDER AS SUSPECT BLOCK.
3. VICTIM'S INJURIES - DETAILS AND WHERE MEDICAL EXAM OCCURRED.
4. PROPERTY DAMAGED - DESCRIBE AND INDICATE AMOUNT OF LOSS.
5. PHYSICAL EVIDENCE - DETAIL WHAT AND WHERE FOUND, BY WHOM, AND DISPOSITION.

6. VEHICLE USED BY SUSPECT AND DISPOSITION.
7. NAME, ADDRESS, PHONE, NUMBER OF JUVENILE'S PARENTS/GUARDIAN(S), NOTE IF
   CONTACTED AND IF INCIDENT ADJUSTED.
8. LIST STATEMENTS TAKEN AND DISPOSITION.
9. RECONSTRUCT INCIDENT AND DESCRIBE INVESTIGATION.
10. OUTLINE TESTIMONY OF PERSONS MARKED "HAS USABLE TESTIMONY" ON FRONT.

5   ITEM #1   ONE TAURUS .38 SPECIAL SERIAL NUMBER KC53213. THE GUN WAS RECOVERED AT THE SCENE

BY OFFICER PAIGE AND SUBMITTED INTO THE EVIDENCE SECTION FOR SAFEKEEPING BY

OFFICER PAIGE.

ITEM #2   ONE BERETTA .380 SERIAL NUMBER D11334Y. THE GUN WAS RECOVERED AT THE LISTED

RESIDENCE BY OFFICER PAIGE AND SUBMITTED INTO SAFEKEEPING BY OFFICER PAIGE.

PRIMARY OFFICER	SERIAL	UNIT	SECONDARY OFFICER	SERIAL	UNIT	APPROVING OFFICER	SER.
E. E. EDWARDS #5726		442	C. PAIGE #5572	CP VWR-0042		HCollen	7P

94-123078

ITEM OR ENTRY	CONTINUATION SHEET (1) INCIDENT	INCIDENT NUMBER 94-123078 UNIT FILE NUMBER

5 CONT. ITEM #3 TAURUS .380 PT 58 ss SERIAL NUMBER KLA69796. THE GUN WAS RECOVERED AT THE LISTED RESIDENCE BY OFFICER PAIGE AND SUBMITTED INTO THE EVIDENCE SECTION FOR SAFE-KEEPING BY OFFICER PAIGE.

ITEM #4 ONE COLT ar-15 SRI SERIAL NUMBER SP 113805. THE GUN WAS RECOVERED AT THE LISTED RESIDENCE BY OFFICER PAIGE AND SUBMITTED INTO THE EVIDENCE SECTION FOR SAFE-KEEPING BY OFFICER PAIGE.

ITEM #5 25 BOXES OF ASSORTED .223, .380, AND .38 ROUNDS. THE ROUNDS OF AMMUNITION WERE RECOVERED AT THE LISTED RESIDENCE BY OFFICER PAIGE AND SUBMITTED INTO THE EVIDENCE SECTION FOR SAFEKEEPING BY OFFICER PAIGE.

ITEM #6 ONE BOTTLE OF ASSORTED, UNIDENTIFIED PILLS. THE PILLS WERE RECOVERED FROM THE PERSON OF COBAIN, KURT WHILE INVESTIGATING THIS INCIDENT. I RECOVERED THE PILLS AND PLACED THE PILLS INTO THE CUSTODY OF OFFICER PAIGE WHO PLACED THE PILLS INTO THE EVIDENCE SECTION FOR SAFEKEEPING.

9   ON THE LISTED DATE AND TIME OFFICERS RESPONDED TO THE LISTED LOCATION TO INVESTIGATE A DISTURBANCE. I ARRIVED AND CONTACTED ▮▮▮▮▮▮▮▮▮▮▮▮ ▮▮▮▮▮▮▮▮ STATED THAT COBAIN, KURT HAD LOCKED HIMSELF IN A ROOM AND THAT HE WAS GOING TO KILL HIMSELF. SHE ALSO STATED THAT HE HAD A GUN IN THE ROOM. OFFICERS WERE ABLE TO CONTACT COBAIN, KURT AND DETAINED HIM PENDING FURTHER INVESTIGATION. COBAIN, KURT STATED THAT HE HAD LOCKED HIMSELF IN THE ROOM TO KEEP AWAY FROM ▮▮▮▮▮▮▮▮ HE CONTINUED TO STATE THAT HE IS NOT SUICIDAL AND DOESN'T WANT TO HURT HIMSELF.

▮▮▮▮▮▮ INFORMED OFFICERS OF THE LOCATION OF SEVERAL WEAPONS THAT WERE IN THE ROOM THAT COBAIN, KURT HAD LOCKED HIMSELF IN. DUE TO THE VOLATILE SITUATION WITH THE THREAT OF SUICIDE AND THE RECOVERY OF UNKNOWN MEDICATION, THE WEAPONS AND MEDICATION WERE INTO CUSTODY. AFTER FURTHER INTERVIEWING ▮▮▮▮ ▮▮▮▮ STATED THAT SHE DID NOT SEE HIM WITH A GUN, AND HE DID NOT SAY HE WAS GOING TO KILL HIMSELF. HOWEVER WHEN HE LOCKED HIMSELF IN THE ROOM, WOULD NOT OPEN THE DOOR, AND KNOWING THAT HE HAD ACCESS TO GUNS, SHE CONTACTED 911 FOR HIS SAFETY AND WELLBEING. ALL PARTIES WERE INTERVIEWED AND RELEASED AND COBAIN, KURT LEFT ▮▮▮ ▮▮▮ THE DISTURBANCE WAS VERBAL ONLY.

INVESTIGATING OFFICER	SERIAL	UNIT	INVESTIGATING OFFICER	SERIAL	UNIT	APPROVING OFFICER
E. E. EDWARDS	#5728	442	C. PAIGE	#5572	442	Robinson 317

*Cobain domestic violence police report. The police found Kurt hiding from Courtney.

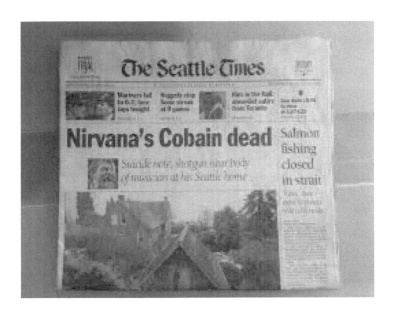

*Many people close to Kurt insist that the Nirvana singer was not suicidal and had made plans to leave Courtney and start a new life.

Kurt Cobain's troubled last days

rugs, guns
id threats;
id then he
sappeared

*Many media outlets described Kurt's last days as being suicidal, without knowing the truth that Kurt wanted to divorce Courtney and start anew. The Cobains had a prenup - Courtney would have not received a penny if they divorced.

FROM COBAIN'S WALLET
4/13/94 CAIS SK 3356

*Note found in Kurt's wallet mocking Courtney

Kurt's Timeline
(from Burntout)

- Born Kurt Donald Cobain on 20th Febuary 1967.
- Born at Grays Habor Community Hospital, Hoquiam, Washington USA.
- Parents Donald and Wendy Cobain.

- Moved to Aberdeen, Washington USA when 6 mths old.

- Sister born three years later, Kimberly Cobain.

- Attended Robert Gray Kindergarten.

- Attended Aberdeen Junior High School.
- In Year 8 he transferred to Miller Junior High School.

- In 1983 transferred to Aberdeen High School.

- Chris Novoselic and Kurt meet at Aberdeen High School.

- In 1986 Kurt recorded fourtrack demo 'fecal matter' with Chris on bass and Aaron Burkhart on drums.

- 1988 Nirvana formed, group

consisted of Kurt, Chris, Chad Channing and Jason Everman.
- 1988 Nirvana signed to Seattle label 'Subpop'.
- Lovebuzz - Big Cheese released as a limited edition of 1000.
- Nirvana recorded Bleach Bleach - CD-Albumfor only $600 in 1988, and was released on 'Subpop' in 1989.

- In 1989 Jason Everman left Nirvana.

- In 1990 Chad Channing left the band, and a Nirvana tour US with dale Crover on drums.
- Sliver was released in 1990

with Mudhoneys Dan Peters
on drums.
- Dave Grohl joins in 1990.
- They signed to Geffen
Records in 1990.

- 1991 Nevermind Nevermind
- Japan - Vinyl-Album
Nevermind - CD-Album
Nevermind - Vinyl-Albumwas
released.

- 24th Febuary,1992 Kurt
married Courney Love.
- Frances Bean was born on
the 18th August 1992, 3 weeks
premature.
- Late 1992 Incestocide was
released.

- Utero was released in 1993.

- April 1994 Kurt died, his body was found dead April 8th 1994 at his Seattle home.

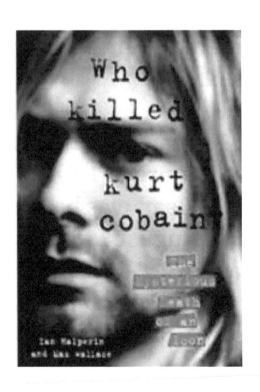

*Courtney tried hard to stop the publication of my first two books.

Michael Stipe, lead singer REM, inducted Nirvana into the Rock and Roll Hall of Fame on April 10, 2014.

Nirvana

At the PNE Forum on Monday, January 3

• BY RON YAMAUCHI

It's good to guess wrong sometimes. In the case of Nirvana, it's nice to be wrong on a consistent basis.

Upon hearing *Nevermind* for the first time, I assumed that Kurt Cobain's talents as a bandleader and composer, however formidable, were so eccentric that his band would never rise above a medium-obscure level of cultish fandom such as that enjoyed by Paul Westerberg. Instead, "Smells Like Teen Spirit" became an enormous hit and Cobain was suddenly a mainstream cultural icon.

The ensuing media frenzy led me to predict that Nirvana would become decadent, declining into self-parody and eventual self-extinction and winding up in the "Early '90s" curio exhibit at the Smithsonian, along with plaid shirts, Ecstasy, and that Davison guy from *The Crying Game*. Instead, the band closed ranks, hardened its outlook even more, and released *In Utero*, a vital but extremely jarring work by musicians who were intent, most of all, on proclaiming their ability to change despite the inhibiting effects of mass success.

On Monday night, I grimly anticipated a show full of "real" but unlistenable aggression and confrontation, with Cobain ranting about his artistic independence and refusing to play the singles. As it turned out, Cobain was shy and said very little, and the band put on an animated and generous set, including "Teen Spirit" and other international anthems. Aided by a second guitarist and a cellist, the band members revealed themselves to be stage pros, playing with great verve but keeping the arrangements as originally written. A "straight" Nirvana is

Neither debauched nor declamatory, Nirvana's pajama-clad Kurt Cobain led his band through a surprisingly tight PNE Forum set. Kevin Statham photo.

perhaps the most surprising of all.

More overt shocks were had via the openers. The Chokebors, from San Francisco, are nontraditional thrashers. Rather than merely playing as fast and loud as possible, they take an intellectual approach, setting up standard verse/chorus structures, then rendering them unrecognizable with exotic *taiko*-like textures and oddball tunings. The resulting cacophony is about as dense, abstract, and dissonant as pop music can get.

The Butthole Surfers are compara-

tively simple musically (a twang version of Skinny Puppy) but far more problematic in terms of presentation. The evil Texans played without lights, dimly backlit by a screen onto which 16mm projectors displayed a variety of dingy, sepia-toned movie loops, including Bruce Lee fights, collapsing bridges, and an assortment of rotting genitalia, many in advanced stages of syphilis. Due to a thrown cigarette, the proceedings were terminated prematurely—perhaps mercifully. Amazement followed. ■

*Nirvana's Live Concerts Took The World By Storm in The Nineties.

Nirvana Singer Found Dead

Kurt Cobain's Fatalism Touched a Generation

By Richard Harrington
and Richard Leiby
Washington Post Staff Writers

Kurt Cobain, who led the grunge band Nirvana to superstardom yet reviled his own success, was found shot in the head at his Seattle home yesterday, an apparent suicide.

By virtue of Nirvana's stunning record sales and MTV exposure, Cobain, 27, was pressured to speak for a youth subculture whose fatalistic outlook was forged by the dissolution of family, lowered expectations in the job market, and endemic drug abuse and violence.

Cobain, the group's lead singer, guitarist and songwriter, had canceled Nirvana's European tour and was at home recovering from a drug and alcohol overdose that had left him in a coma in Rome last month. His body was discovered by an electrician, with a shotgun and a long, single-page suicide note nearby, Seattle police said. Cobain had not been seen in six days; his body, found in an apartment above a detached garage, had been there about a day, according to police. The last two lines of the note read, "I love you. I love you," the electrician, Gary Smith, said in an interview on Los Angeles television station KNBC.

In 1991, Nirvana helped create and define a category of guitar-driven rock—grunge—through the hit song "Smells Like Teen Spirit." The band's breakthrough pushed underground rock music into the mainstream. A mix of punk and pop influences, grunge sparked a fashion craze of flannel shirts and Doc Martens boots and resulted in a wave of cult bands being signed by major labels.

■ For fans of the rock star, his death amplifies their despair. Page B1

Grunge rock star Kurt Cobain seemed an authentic disciple of the no-future punk aesthetic.

Nirvana's "Nevermind" album sold 10 million copies worldwide, a staggering accomplishment Cobain recoiled upon as the first line of the

See COBAIN, A16, Col. 1

Smells like ...?

Suspicions abound that Kurt Cobain's death wasn't what Seattle police claim

Made in United States
Troutdale, OR
02/16/2024